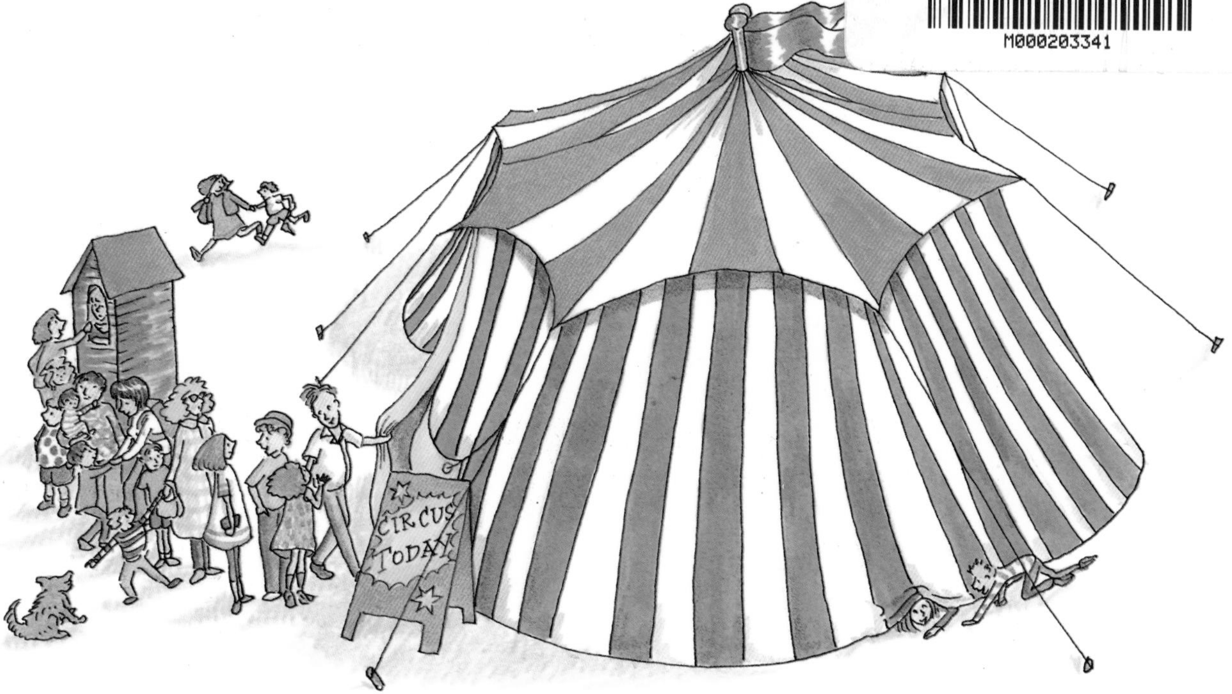

We can see a tent.

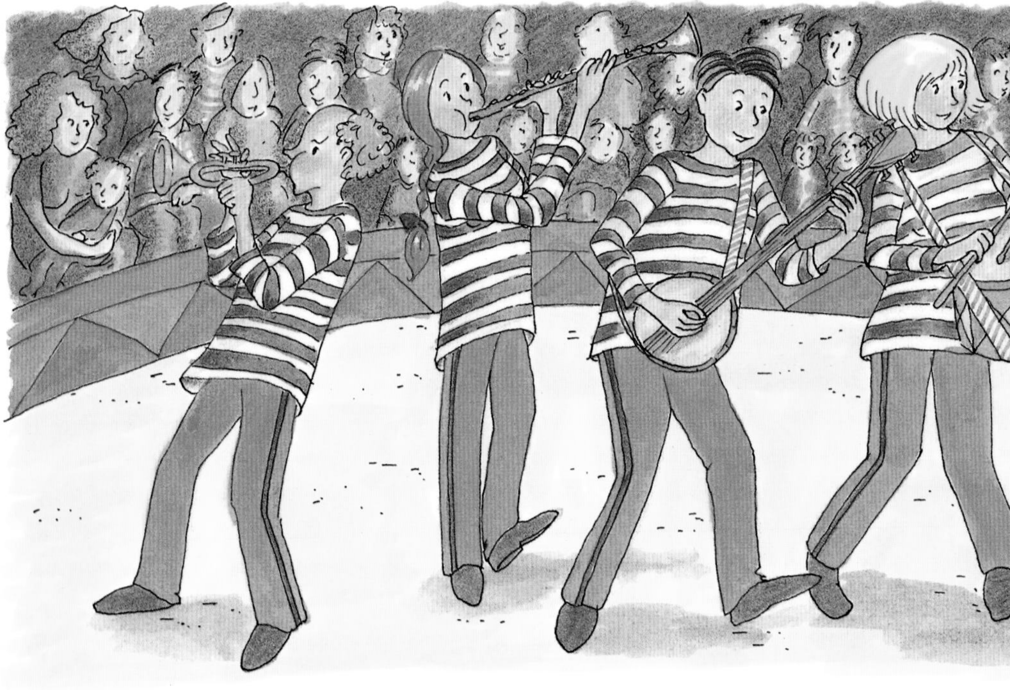

We can see a band.

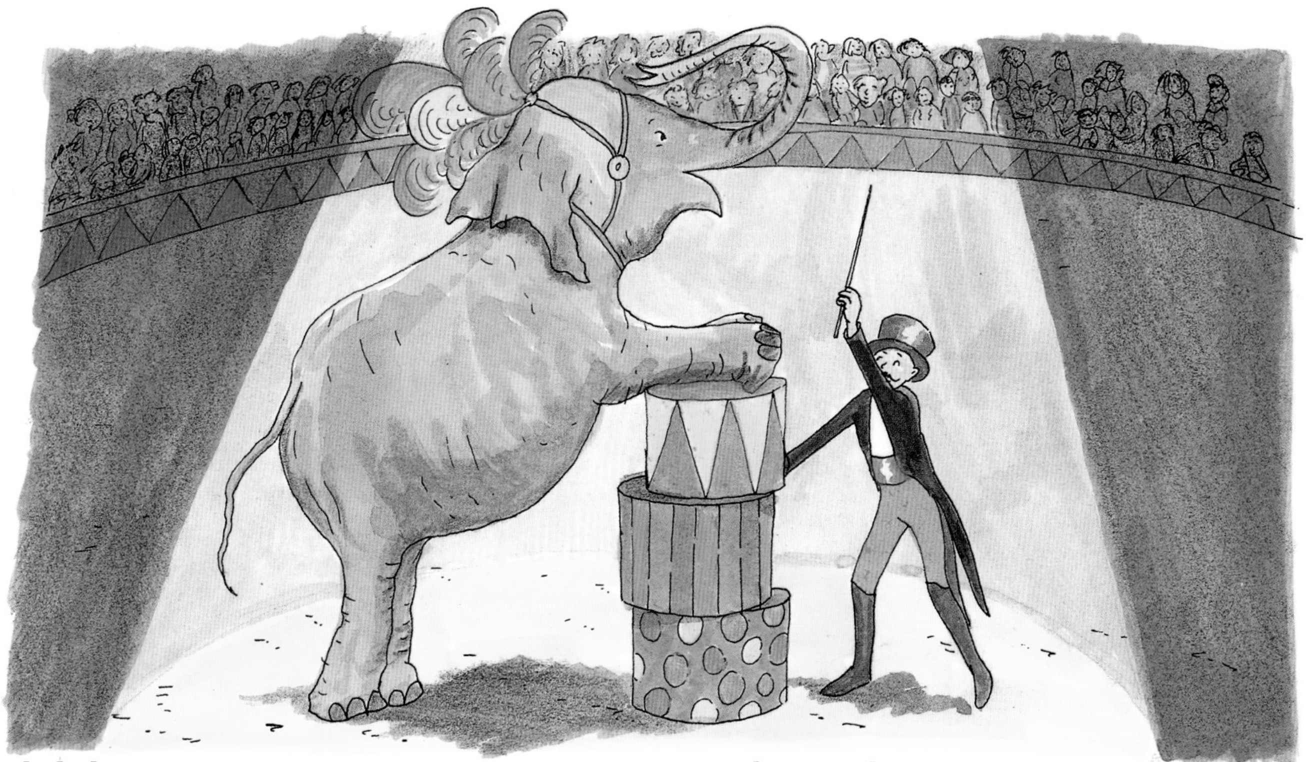

We can see an elephant.

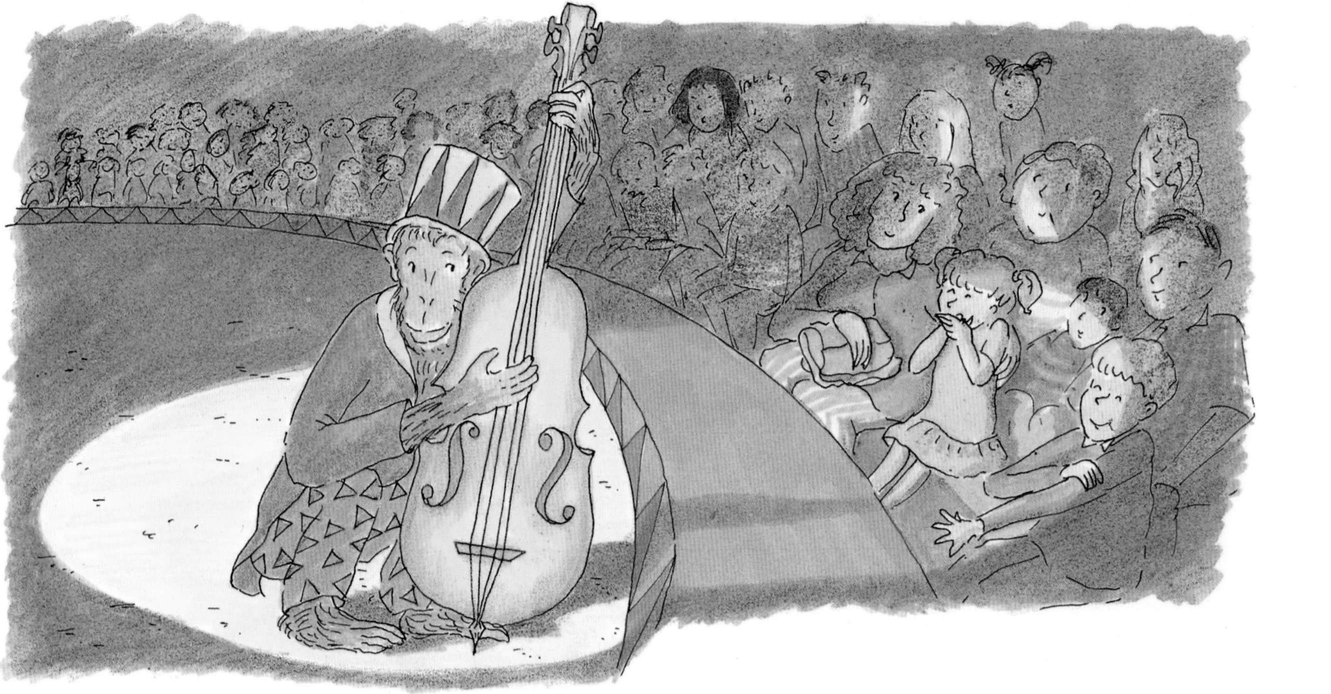

We can see a monkey.

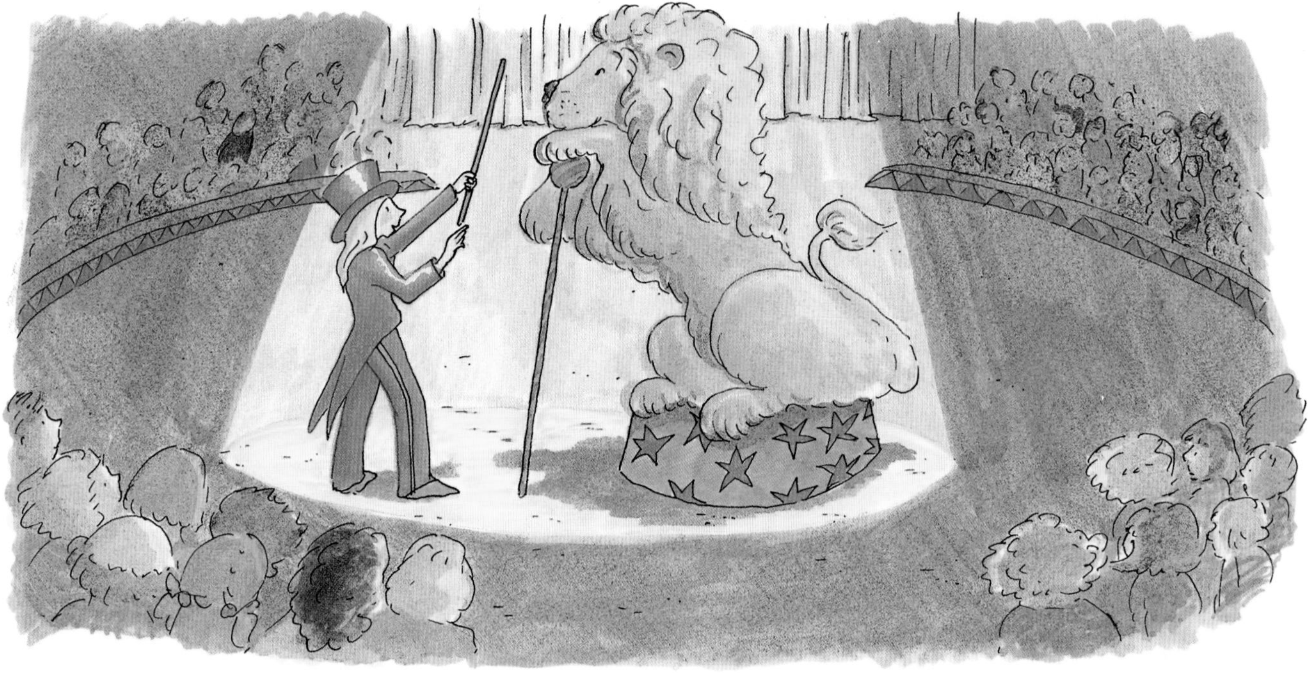

We can see a lion.

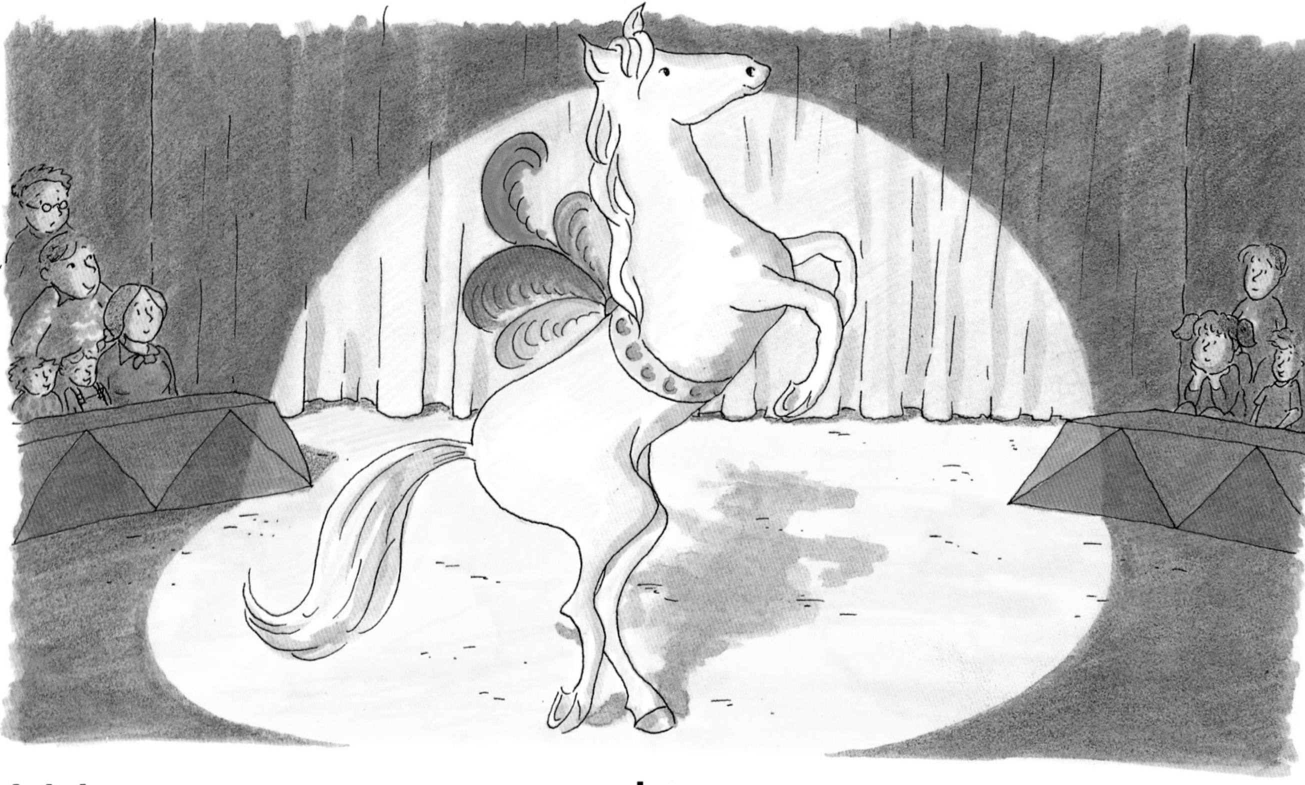

We can see a horse.

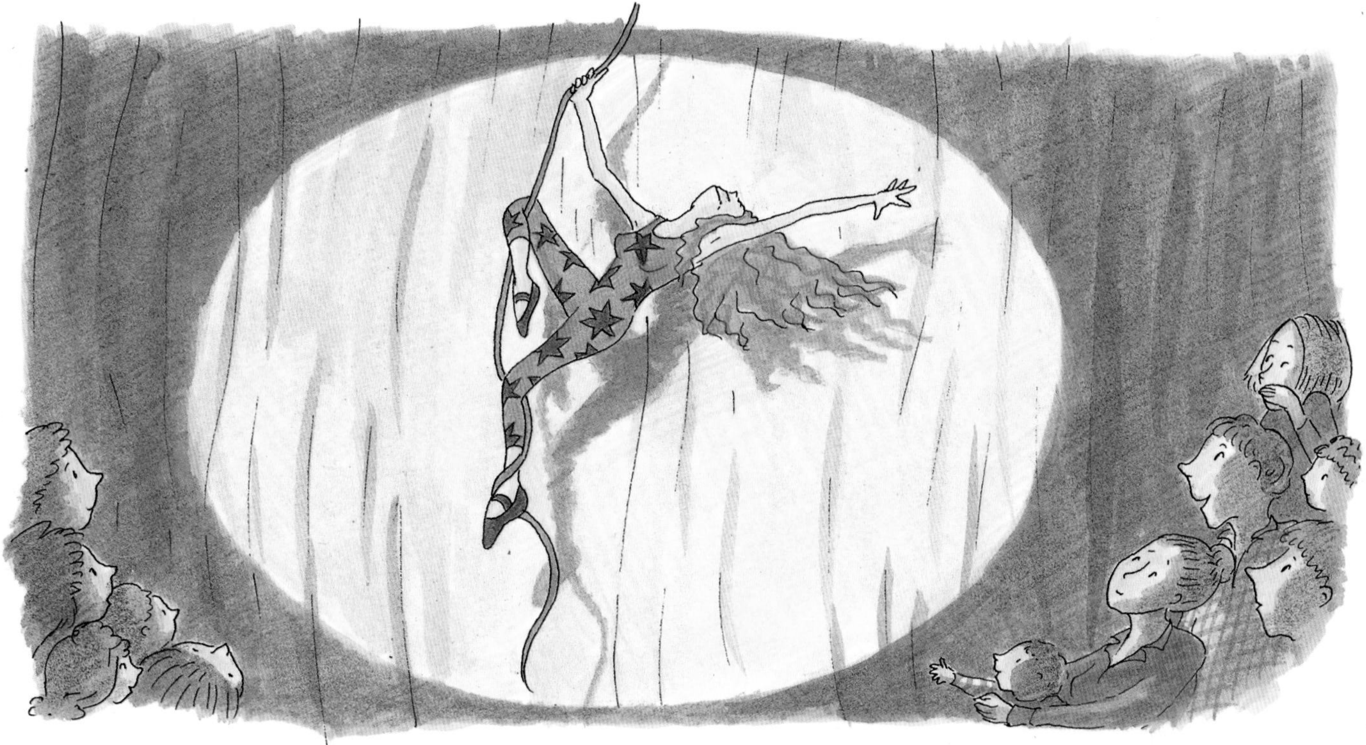

We can see an acrobat.

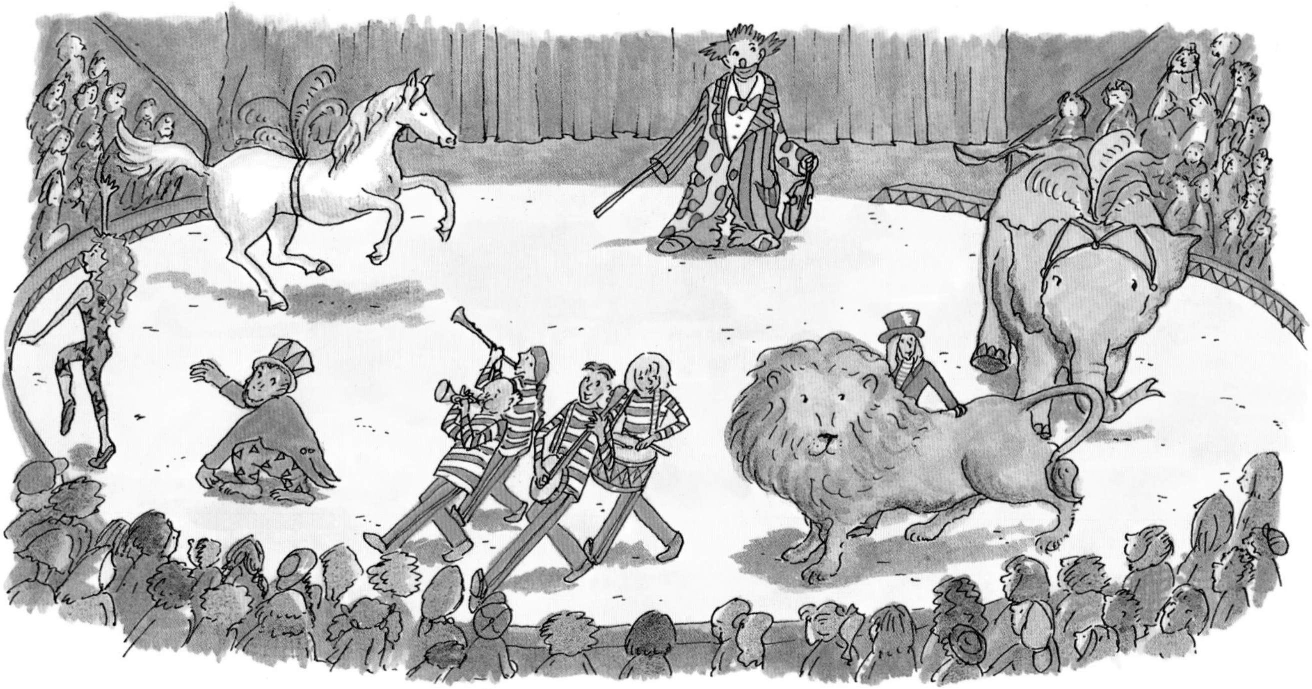

We can see a clown.